# Things Mama Used to Say

## LYNN BROWN

Hope of Vision Publishing
Bridgeport, Connecticut

Things Mama Used to Say
Copyright © 2014 by Lynn Brown

Unless otherwise specified, all Scripture quotations in this book are from The Holy Bible, King James Version. KJV is Public domain in the United States printed in 1987. NCV Bible online.

Hope of Vision Publishing a division of HOV, LLC.
www.hopeofvisionpublishing.com
hopeofvision@gmail.com

Editor: Phyllis Bridges

Cover Design: Brian Collier
Back Cover Photo Credit:
Vernesia King (Liz) All About You Photos

For more information about special discounts for bulk purchases, please contact Hope of Vision Publishing.

ISBN 978-1-6203089-2-9

Printed in the United States of America

# DEDICATION

1 Chronicles 4:9-10

9 And Jabez was more honourable than his brethren: and his mother called his name Jabez, saying, Because I bare him with sorrow.

10 And Jabez called on the God of Israel, saying, Oh that thou wouldest bless me indeed, and enlarge my coast, and that thine hand might be with me, and that thou wouldest keep me from evil, that it may not grieve me! And God granted him that which he requested.

And I, like Jabez, was born in pain. The story goes – Daddy was an alcoholic and while under the influence daddy he hit

Momma in the head with a plate and kicked her in the stomach.

Nevertheless, I was born with two teeth and a veil over my face and three days after I went home. While Momma was holding me she was eating cornbeef hash and I decided that I wanted some too, so I reached my hand into her plate and started eating. Well the rest is history.

This book is dedicated to my sisters and brothers, Bennie Jr., Annie, Harry, Melvina, John, Diane, Larry and Michelle. In memory of our Mother, who left an everlasting impression upon us and has sustained us for the last 14 years that she has been absent from our lives.

I dedicate this book to the woman who inspired it all. She has influenced my life greatly, molded and taught me how to be a fighter and to never give up. Momma this book is for you! I want the world to know everything that you used to teach me and my sisters and brothers.

I Love you Lois Ann Lockhart-Jackson

# ACKNOWLEDGEMENT

To whom Much is given, Much is required. First and foremost, I want to give honor to God, who is the Head of my life. He is the true author and creator and I am just a vessel; willing to be used by Him. Thank you for using me.

To you, Harry O, I want to say thank you for all that you have done for me. When I met you, it was at a time when I was not sure where I wanted to go. Thank you for giving me a dose of reality, and for pushing me into my destiny. It is because of you that I wrote this book. You were the fuel to my fire in many ways and still are and I love you for that.

To the three most important men in my life, I want to say thank you for putting up with me and loving me for my good, bad, ugly and indifferences. I love you with all of my heart, mind and soul. Earnest, Adrian and Kevin Thompson, you have been that sustaining joy in my life.

To my two side-kicks, my ride or die chicks, Kimberley Hamilton and Tasha Davis-Burton; you have been there for me and just when I got weak and felt like I could fall; the two of you were right there to catch me. Kim, I constantly hear you saying, "God Got You".

To my girlfriends for life, Leah Gibson, Bridget Miller, Cheryl Robinson, Ramona Graham, Karen Smith-Brown, Janet West, Natasha Jones and Verniesa Liz King; the hard work has paid off. It's time for a girls night out on the town.

---

# CONTENTS

1. Yo' Eyes Bigga Than Yo' Belly.......... 13
2. Too Smart For Your Own Damn Good . 14
3. If You Like It ...……………………….... 15
4. A Pot to Piss In ……………………...... 17
5. This Gone Hurt Me ……………………. 18
6. Go Get That Switch Off The Tree ....... 21
7. Sittin On Your Ass ………………….....22
8. You Never Know Until You Try ......... 23
9. Give Me My Flowers …………………. 24
10. Don't Put Off Today …………………. 26
11. There Is More Than One Way …………27
12. If You Look …...……………………... 29
13. Feed Them With A Long Handle
     Spoon …………………………….…… 30
14. A Little Pain Never Killed Anybody .... 31
15. Ain't No Need Of Crying ……………...32
16. Can't See The Forest For The Trees ….. 33
17. I Will Lift …...……………………….... 34
18. A Man Ain't Nothing But A Dog ….….. 35
19. Don't Put All Your Eggs In One

Basket ..................................... 36
20. Always Save For A Rainy Day ........... 37
21. The Bigger They Are The Harder
    They Fall ....................................38
22. A Still Tongue Totes A Wise Head ...... 39
23. Don't Bite Off More Than You Can
    Chew ..................................... 40
24. Don't Put The Cart Before the Horse .. 41
25. Fas Ass .............................................. 42
26. I'm The Parent You're The Child ...... 44
27. A Dog Who Brings A Bone, Will
    Carry A Bone .............................45
28. Don't Nothing Get Old .................... 46
29. Every Man Who Smiles In Your
    Face ........................................ 47
30. Sometimes You Got To Pray For
    Yo Self ...................................... 48
31. You Were Not Born In A Monkey
    Suit .......................................... 49
32. Seldom Visits Make Better Friends ...... 50
33. The Early Bird Catches The Worm ..... 51
34. One Monkey Don't Stop No Show........ 52
35. You Are Better Off Trying Jesus ........ 53
36. If You Play With A Dog He Will Lick

You In The Mouth ........................... 54

37. If You Wallow with Dogs You Will
    Get Up With Fleas ............................  55
38. I'm Gonna Slap The Living Taste
    Outcha Mouth ............................... 56
39. Oh Come and See Ain't Like Old Stay
    Together ...................................... 57
40. Tell It Like It "I" "S" Is ................... 58
41. 6 Months ..................................... 59
42. Can't See Your Hands ..................... 60
43. Don't Let The Green Grass Fool Ya ..... 61
44. I'm Gonna Beat You Like White
    On Rice ......................................  62
45. I Mean What I Say ..........................  63
46. I Got Eyes ...................................  65
47. Shittin in High Cotton and Wiping
    with the Blooms ............................. 66
48. Sorry Didn't Do It ......................... 67
49. I'm Gonna Cut You ......................... 69
50. Watch As Well As Pray ................... 70
51. For The Old And The New ............... 71
52. That's Yo Lil' Red Wagon ............... 73
53. Laziness Hugging and Kissing You ...... 74
54. The Lord Will ............................... 75

55. If You Don't Sit Down ........................ 77
56. Fair Weather Friends ......................... 78
57. The Black Woman .............................. 79
About The Author .......................................... 83
Photo Album ............................................... 85

## *Yo' Eyes Bigga Than Yo' Belly*

---

I remember one summer my oldest sister and her husband came down from Orlando, FL to drop off my niece, Kim and her brother, Von. The first night there my Momma made a huge pot of spaghetti and my brother, Larry, decided that he was going to show out and fix himself a huge plate. He yelled out to everybody that he could eat a horse, my mother told him it was way too much for him, but he did not want to listen.

So about 10 minutes into Larry eating his food he yelled out, "I'm full, I need to go to the bathroom." My mother said to him, "Take your plate with you, cause while you are putting in you can be pushing out; now that should teach you about having eyes bigga than yo belly."

---

## *Too Smart For Your Own Damn Good*

Trickery and foolery were not in my Mother's vocabulary. She did not believe in raising disrespectful children. As a matter of fact, wherever you showed out, is where you were corrected.

Whenever company came over, usually my Aunt Essie and Aunt Mel, you had better find something to do or be in a child's place until company left. You better not get caught up in grown folk's conversations, that was the quickest way to get backhand-slapped across the face; without Momma even looking at you. Now after she slapped you, she would tell you "Learn to stay in a child's place, a child ain't got no business being in adult conversation; you're just too smart for your own damn good!"

## *If You Like It*

---

I remember when my sister, Diane, was dating this professional boxer who qualified for the lightweight division. Well one Friday night he jumped on my sister and she called Momma to come to her rescue.

Momma never walked anywhere, but on that particular night my mom showed me just how much she loved her children and especially my sister. Diane did not know that she was Momma's favorite.

Momma said to me and my niece, Kim, "Y'all come on and go with me to Diane's house. Diane lived in Madison Apartments, aka The Greens because of their color. When we arrived Momma did not mince any words, she was straight to the point. She looked the boxer straight in the eyes and

---

said, "If you ever lay hands on my daughter again you won't have to worry about the police coming, you'll need to worry about the ambulance taking your ass to the hospital or morgue." The boxer was astonished at what my mother said to him. She then turned back to my sister and made herself crystal clear, she said:

*I know your ass is gonna go right back to him but understand one thing if you do, don't call me, I won't interfere; because I know that you and him will end up together again. So if you like those ass whoopings, I love it. I can't pick and choose who you gonna date or marry but don't put me in harm's way.*

That night on the way back home my mother made a vow to never interfere in any of her children's relationships again.

## *A Pot to Piss In*

Mother was always one to give positive words of kindness and affirmations; she believed in the word humility because that was her demeanor. She was always offering you a plate of food, and sometimes she might even open up her doors to give you a place to lay your head. But if you thought you had come up or arrived at a place in your life where you thought that you were all of that and you called yourself getting your ass on your shoulders, she would just look at you and say, you ain't even got "*A pot to piss in* nor a window to throw it out of."

## *This Gone Hurt Me*

---

Now I love this one, sometimes I still try to figure out why? I can remember on several occasions when I got caught doing something wrong and Lois Ann was not in the mood to whoop me. Especially on this particular occasion when I was about 13 years old and there was these three boys who liked me, two of them were brothers and the other one was their best friend. Well this is how the story goes, they made a bet on which one of them I would choose to date, and it's sad to see when guys are sore losers.

I chose the best friend, instead of one of the brothers. So the brothers decided that they would come up with a lie to tell my mom that I skipped school with their best friend. Well they came knocking on my

---

mother's door and told her this information unbeknownst to me, so when I came home from school after band practice as soon as I walked in the door my mother said, "I am only gonna ask you one time and you better tell me the truth, did you skip school today." Of course my reply was "No M'am." Well that did not fly with her. She looked at me with the belt in hand and said, "I gave you the opportunity to come clean and since you did not, well *this is gonna hurt* me more than it will hurt you." The two brothers knew that my mom was very strict and did not play the radio and had set me up. After she whooped me, she asked for details. When I told her what was going on she said, "Well sometimes you have to give up the right for the wrong." I decided I would give it up for the moment, but the next day you know those two brothers had it coming. I was notorious for beating up people if you

did something to me. Well just so you know
those two brothers never told another
lie on me again.

## *Go Get That Switch Off The Tree*

---

There is nothing worse than being told to go get the switch off the tree, which will be used to inflict pain upon you. African American parents are notorious for asking you to assist them in your own punishment in hopes of persuading their kids from being bad. That's just like saying dig your own grave. No child wants to get their own switch that will be used to beat them from off the tree.

Let's take a look at this request. First of all, you caught me doing wrong; next you feel as a part of the punishment I need to get my own switch and then give it to you to beat me with. Really Mom? I could never rationalize this punishment until I had kids of my own. All I can say now is that it worked.

---

## *Sittin On Your Ass*

---

This was my mom's all-time favorite saying. She had a sign hanging over her front door with a man sitting on a donkey that read: "*Sitting On Your Ass* and Worrying Ain't Gone Get You No Where." So no matter who you were or where you came from if you entered my Mother's home her departing words to you would be the above statement.

---

## *You Never Know Until You Try*

---

Can't was a word that was not allowed in Lois Ann Lockhart-Jackson's home. If you wanted to get under her skin, come in talking about how worried you are, or you can't do this or that. She was quick to tell you, *"You never know until you try."* If you were not willing to try, then don't complain.

---

## *Give Me My Flowers*

---

My Mother was a very special lady. She always had kind words for anyone who crossed her path. Every Sunday morning my mother made it her business to have breakfast ready for the entire family. She made cooking seem so easy. The first to arrive every Sunday morning was my brother, Harry; with a rose in hand. It seemed as if Mother Frances knew on cue when to play "This Faded Rose" by Shirley Caesar.

In the beginning of the song Shirley begins to tell a story of a young man who moved to Germany and while there he was injured, and the doctors told him he would never walk again. Well as the young man walked to the fresh grave of his mother, he began to drop rose peddles on her grave.

---

Shirley said as the young man dropped the pedals these are the words he said:

*Peddles from this faded roses Momma, is all I have to give, but Momma I tried to give you flowers, every now and then. If I had a million dollars, I would line your grave with gold, but wouldn't wake you from your sleep, as eternal ages grow. So peddles from this faded rose is all I have to give. But Momma I tried to make you happy, while you lived.*

Every time my mother would hear this song, she and my brother would embrace and start crying. She would tell him, "Just *give me my flowers* while I yet live because once the roof of my mouth turns blue, there will be no need to give me flowers when I'm dead and gone."

## Don't Put Off Today

---

Momma did not like procrastination, if she told you to do something, she very well meant for it to be done as soon as you were given the order or instruction. She would say, "*Don't put off today* for tomorrow because it ain't promised to you."

---

## *There Is More Than One Way*

---

I was the child who always had to try my mother's patience and if she was here today she would tell you that. I always found a way to bend the rules to work in my favor based on her teachings. Momma was very strict with her girls and she made sure we understood that we had that we worked for whatever we wanted in life.

I realized that if I wanted to get certain things, I had to figure out how to get around her saying no to me and then use what she taught me. Because like she said, "There is more than one way to skin a cat." So to circumvent her telling me no when I wanted to go out with my friends or attend certain events or activities, I decided to join many of the school's clubs and sports teams. Such as R.O.T.C., Band, DECA and track, which

---

allowed me to attend the football and basketball games, and pep rallies.

## *If You Look*

---

This saying is so true, I remember once I was dating this guy and I had this gut feeling that something in the milk was not clean. So I sought the advice of my mother and she told me:

*Baby if you look for trouble you will find it, but if you just wait on the Lord, He will reveal it because what goes on in the dark will come to the light. Just ask God and He will reveal it, but only when He thinks that you can handle it; but when you look you will find more than you bargained for.*

---

## *Feed Them With A Long Handle Spoon*

---

In life you will have friends, enemies, frienemies and family that act just like the enemy. Momma told us there are some people and family who will lie, steal and cheat; they are just like snakes in the grass.

Once you find out who they are, it does not mean you have to dismiss them but keep them at a distance. Because just like the snake if you are not careful, they will sneak up on you and bite. Feed him with a long handle spoon. Don't let them get close enough to bite you or be in your business.

---

## *A Little Pain Never Killed Anybody*

In life there are circumstances and situations that will arise and cause pain and suffering.

Mom would tell us that there would be days like this..... and pain and suffering are to be expected. She would also remind us that "A little pain never hurt anybody, but dwelling in it will."

## *Ain't No Need Of Crying*

---

In life sometimes we make some mistakes, or we realize that we can't retract our steps in a situation that could have been prevented, then we start crying shoulda, woulda, coulda and Mama would yell out, "*Ain't no need* of crying over spilled milk." She said, "You have to pick up, keep it moving and stop wallowing in self-pity." Go back to the Cow with your pail and get yourself a fresh batch of milk.

---

## *Can't See The Forest For The Trees*

---

Have you ever looked for something and it was right there in your face or have you looked at a situation and you could not see what was really happening? When we would get stupid with life's situations and couldn't see what was really happening before us, Momma didn't have a problem telling us, "You *can't see the forest for the trees*," because we were being too ignorant. She hated stupidity. What mother meant by that, is that we are too busy looking at the situation, rather than looking beyond the situation for solutions.

---

## *I Will Lift*

Psalms 121

---

*I will lift* up mine eyes unto the hills, from whence cometh my help. My help *cometh* from the Lord… You could not walk into my Mother's house and not hear these words. She woke up every morning saying these words, which continued on every noon day and every night before she went to bed quoting this scripture. My Sisters and brothers knew that this was her motto and anyone she encountered they learned very fast that all her help came from the Lord.

---

## *A Man Ain't Nothing But A Dog*

My mother and her baby sister, Kate, would be sitting around talking and having their daily discussion when all of a sudden my Aunt Kate would bust out and say, "A man a nothing but a dog". I used to sit and wonder why she would say that, until one day what she was saying dawned on me. Then a thought occurred to me if *"A man ain't nothing but a dog,"* then there must just be different breeds. Just be careful of the dog you bring home, because you might come up with flees.

## Don't Put All Your Eggs In One Basket

---

I can remember applying for a job and I was so sure that I got the job. When I did not get the job my Mom said, "Baby never *put all your eggs in one basket*, you are only setting yourself up for disappointment."

---

## *Always Save For A Rainy Day*

---

You never know when hard times are gonna happen, you should at least have three months of savings or something saved for emergencies; because you can't depend on others to bail you out of your situations or circumstances. Momma drilled in us that you must *"Always save for a rainy day."*

---

## **The Bigger They Are**
## **The Harder They Fall**

---

I was small in size, but I was notorious for fighting. It was so bad that my eldest brother, whom we affectionately called Bo-Peep, nick named me Devil.

My reason for being so mean was most people underestimated me because of my size. So Momma would tell me "Don't worry about the size of a man/woman just remember *the bigger they are, the harder they will fall*." She said that if the person is bigger than you never reach up to fight them, go straight for the knee caps, if you hit them in the knee they have to drop down to your size, then knock the living daylights out of them.

---

## *A Still Tongue Totes A Wise Head*

---

Due to my quick temper Momma was constantly repeating this to me, there were a lot of times when I would find myself in situations and because I was so quick tempered I would be ready to fire off at someone and tell them what I felt, and especially if I was correct, I would want to let them know what time it was and the fact that they were incorrect. Momma would tell me, "Baby you don't always need to let people know that you are right and you can't always let the left hand know what the right hand is doing; sometimes you need to keep the enemy guessing." Her most famous quote to us was *"A still tongue totes a wise head."*

---

# Don't Bite Off More Than You Can Chew

A lot of times you can find yourselves in situations where you have said yes you'll do something, and then you realize that it is overwhelming; but you don't know how to tell the individual that it is too much, or you don't know how to back out of the situation. Understand that there is nothing wrong with saying No; but you should have a problem saying Yes. So, Momma would tell us *"Don't bite off more than you can chew."*

## Don't Put The Cart Before the Horse

There were a lot of times when we wanted to do something and we'd get all excited about the idea. We wanted to run full speed ahead before weighing out all of the pros and cons. Momma would tell us "Hold your horses you can't *put the cart before the horse*." "She'd say Momma would say, "Be anxious for nothing."

## *Fas Ass*

---

As I have said throughout this book, "Momma had a way with words." I remember I needed to get a pencil box for school, I am laughing as I tell this story, well Momma and My Aunt Melvina were the Avon queens, and there was this new scent that Avon had produced call Foxfire.

Momma went to Kentucky Fried Chicken and bought each of us our own dinner. Because she would not go to the store that afternoon and get my pencil box, I decided that I would make one using my Kentucky Fried Chicken box. I got some construction paper and covered the box. Then I sprayed the box down with Foxfire perfume, with all of my pencil and pens in it. I put my name on it and I was ready to take it to school the next day.

---

Being a *"Fas Ass"*, as Momma would say, I took the box to school. Every time I opened it, all I could smell was greasy chicken and Foxfire perfume mixed together. Oh my God what a smell! I was soooo nauseous that I did not know what to do. I could not wait to get home and throw the box away.

When I got home my mother asked me what was wrong with me and I told her what I did. She said, "See what I mean, you deserve that always wanting to be a fas ass; but what you did not know is that I bought you the box and if you were not in such a hurry this morning, I would have given it to you."

## *I'm The Parent You're The Child*

---

Too often me and my sisters and brothers heard these words when Mom would chastise us and we would get all flipped mouth with her and dispute her argument. She would quickly remind us with *"I am the Parent and you are the child."* "You can let the door knob hitcha where the good Lawd splitcha."

---

## A Dog Who Brings A Bone, Will Carry A Bone

---

Momma always told us:

*Never trust a person who is always gossiping about another person. You better believe whatever they are telling you about that person or whatever was said about you, you better believe if you say anything about that person, the gossiper will be taking that information back to the person who talked about you. Then when you confront them on it, all of a sudden they have amnesia. So Mom would tell us a dog who brings a bone, will carry one.*

---

## Don't Nothing Get Old

My mother believed in being forever young, you better not come around her acting all old fashion; talking about you're too old for stuff. She would quickly tell you "*Don't nothing get old* but clothes and they come back in style; the bible tells you that there is nothing new under the sun."

## *Every Man Who Smiles In Your Face*

---

We women are good for this... Every time a man smiles at us or gives us attention, we automatically think that he is interested or that he is husband material. Mom had this thing that she would say that *"Every man that smiles in your face* ain't meant to be your husband."

---

## *Sometimes You Got To Pray For Yo Self*

---

My Mother loves her grandkids. Upon her death she had a total of 72 kids, which included kids, grandkids and great-grands. One of her favorites was my nephew, Don Q, as he calls himself. Well, my nephew had a run in with the law and a few days before my mother begged him to come see her. Well, he felt that he would come see her when he got time. Unfortunately, Don Q ran out of time, a few days after my mother's birthday he was arrested. He called my mother collect and when she answered he requested that she pray for him. Momma's reply was "*Sometimes you gotta pray fo yo-self* because God is waiting to hear from you."

---

## *You Were Not Born In A Monkey Suit*

My nephew used to love to climb on the curtains and swing. Momma had to beat his butt all the time. Now that he's a grown man with three sons that look and act just like him, he wants to act all strict with them. But he forgot that while growing up Momma used to tell him "Boy *you were not born in a monkey suit* so stop acting like one."

## *Seldom Visits Make Better Friends*

I can remember playing and hanging out with my cousin and my best friend every day after school. I loved to go over to their house and Momma used to tell me, "You need to stay home sometimes or allow them to come and visit you!" I would get offended and say to Momma, "Those are just my friends and cousins." Momma told me that in time, you will see when they turn on you. I would just brush off what she told me until one day, her words became true. My cousin and I had a major falling out. My Momma quickly told me, *"Seldom visits make better friends."* Every since that situation happened, I have kept this as a rule in my house; you can be my friend, but we won't be hanging out together all the time. You will know when to go home and I will know when to go home.

## *The Early Bird Catches The Worm*

---

My mother was one who believed in rising early in the morning. She was just like the proverbial woman, who rises early in the morning preparing breakfast and fixing my step-dad's lunch. After all the kids moved out, she still made it her business to be up. She always said *"The Early Bird Catches the Worm* and a Successful Man Never Sleeps."

---

## *One Monkey Don't Stop No Show*

---

Let's just say, you had a plan or plans and it was going fine. Out of nowhere, someone or something throws a monkey wrench (obstacle) into your plans. If you would let Momma know, you would definitely hear these words, *"One monkey don't stop no show."* Her philosophy was that what one person won't do, another person will. She believed that when one door closes, another will open.

---

## *You Are Better Off Trying Jesus*

---

I can't speak for the rest of my sisters and brothers and besides by the time it got down to me Momma already knew all the tricks of the trade. So if I thought that I was going to try something and get away with it, she would politely let me know, *"You are better off trying Jesus* than trying me, he got grace and mercy; I don't." So whatever I thought I was gonna get away with, I had another thing coming, but of course you know I tried it anyways.

---

## *If You Play With A Dog He Will Lick You In The Mouth*

---

Momma always felt that a child should stay in a child's place. She also thought that an adult should never play with a child to the extent that the child felt comfortable expressing her/himself without respect for who you were as the adult or parent. She always thought that the child would eventually embarrass you in public.

---

## *If You Wallow with Dogs You Will Get Up With Fleas*

Momma had five girls and she never wanted us to end up with the wrong man. Being the forth youngest girl, I would pay close attention to my three older sisters on who they dated and how they were treated. I also paid close attention to who my brothers dated and how they treated the women they dated. Mom would tell my sisters and brothers to please pay attention to who you date; *"If you wallow with dogs you will get up with fleas."* That was Mom's way of saying for us to protect ourselves when being sexually active.

## *I'm Gonna Slap The Living Taste Outcha Mouth*

---

Mom was the type that if she told you to do something, right then and there you better move. If you tried to give her lip service, my advice to you was not to allow her to get within 10 feet of you; if she did you better start praying and hope that God moves fast enough on your behalf. What was to come next was a backhand slap across the face, which felt like thunder and lighting.

---

## *Oh Come and See Ain't Like Old Stay Together*

Now we all know what it is to court or date someone, but you never really know a person until you have lived with them. So Momma said it was one thing to come and see me, but ain't nothing like living under the same roof. You will know all the good, the bad, the ugly and indifferences. Momma would say, "Ain't nothing like knowing a person's farts." "If you can handle his or her farts, then ya'll will stay together."

## *Tell It Like It "I" "S" Is*

---

As I look back at the things my mother said, this was one that always captivated me. Momma would try to be gentle with you by using positive criticism. If you could not handle it, then she would just let it rip and say *"Tell it like it "I" "S" is."* After she would tell you the bitter truth, she would politely say, "I didn't mean no harm."

---

## *6 Months*

---

Have you ever had people to come into your life who were soooooooooo noisy? They always wanted to be in your business and wanted to fix your life, but their life was so jacked up that they could not even fix their own problems because they were two worried about yours. Mom would say, "God give you *6 months* to tend to your business and 6 months to stay out of other folks business," which meant you have a whole year to fix yours and to work on you.

---

## Can't See Your Hands

You know as kids we always wanted to stay out until it was dark. My brother Larry always broke that rule. My mother would call him by his nickname Butch and say, "If you *can't see your hands* in front of your face then you know it is time to come in." If she had to come looking for you, your soul belonged to her.

## *Don't Let The Green Grass Fool Ya*

How many times in life have you been in a relationship or you saw something new that you wanted and you felt it looked good and you had to have it? So you gave up what you had to get this new thing or person only to realize that what you got was not all that it was cracked up to be. Momma would tell us, "Baby, *don't let the green grass fool ya.*"

## *I'm Gonna Beat You Like White On Rice*

Once again my brother Larry was getting into trouble with Mom, there was not a week that went by when he wasn't getting into trouble. While talking about him, I must say I was just as bad. We were always fighting with my nieces or doing something and she would threaten us and put the fear of God in us. She would tell us, *"I'm gonna beat you like white on rice."* And believe you me that was one whooping you did not want because whenever she got started there was no letting go.

## *I Mean What I Say*

---

I can remember one Friday night I wanted to go out to this party; I asked my Momma if I could go and she told me no. So I went back twenty minutes later and asked again; she looked at me and said, "I said no, now don't ask me anymore." Well, you know I tried her again an hour later; she came back at me and said no again. Well, I decided that I was going to go to that party anyway wearing my brand new jeans that zipped up on the leg. You could not tell me anything, I knew I had it going on. Well, when I made it home my mother was waiting for me. I made a bee-line straight to my bathroom because I had to pee really, really bad. My mom came in right behind me and sat on the toilet, she lectured me for more than an hour and a half until I could not take it anymore. Just as I began to

---

relieve myself in my brand new jeans she looked at me and said, "*I told you I meant what I said* and said what I meant."

## *I Got Eyes*

Just when you thought you had gotten away with the ultimate scheme and Momma did not catch you, she would ask, "Where you been, what you been doing?" And of course you'd come up with a little white lie and Momma would wait until you got all comfortable and then look at you and say "*I got eyes* in the back of my head or 'a little birdie just came and told me what you been doing." Now because of your curious nature you want to know how she found out, so like a little dummy you'd fall into her trap and ask the question– who told you what? Then you start denying, "But I didn't do anything." And Momma would just sit there and shake her head; then she would say "The guilty always speak first, now tell me the truth." Guest what you were busted and you told on yourself.

## *Shittin in High Cotton and Wiping with the Blooms*

This is for all the high and mighty people who think that they are better than anyone else. One week you went to borrow some butter, a cup of sugar, or just maybe a few dollars from Momma. Now this week you're too good to call or just stop by to say you're doing fine, now according to Momma you were considered *"Shittin in High Cotton and Wiping with the Blooms"*

## *Sorry Didn't Do It*

---

Don't ever get caught doing something you had no business doing, then once you're caught the first thing you want to say is I'm sorry. Sorry was a word that was not allowed in our home, Momma would tell us quick "I did not raise no sorry ass children, and don't ever let me hear you say you're sorry because *sorry did not do it*, you did." Now if you wanted to apologize for your action, you could by first of all acknowledging that you did it, and then stating that you did not mean to do it, or simply say I apologize. Any of those options were acceptable. But note, just because you apologized didn't mean that you were excused from your punishment. You had to get your own switch or you could choose the leather belt you wanted to get whooped

---

with. Talking about being sorry, the only thing I was sorry for was getting caught.

## *I'm Gonna Cut You*

---

Let me tell you the story about me and my nieces that I grew up with, Kim and Tasha. Well whenever I would get into one of my selfish moods and did not want to play or share with them my Mother would get really pissed off with me. She had this thing that she would say to me and the other grandkids, or whoever pissed her off at the time and moment when she got to the point where she was tired of us cutting the fool.

I was, as always, notorious for it. I especially remember the time when I told my niece, Tasha, not to touch my baby dolls and I grabbed a rock and hit her in the head with it. Momma grabbed me in the collar and said "*I'm gonna cut you* till you are too short to shit" that was enough for me to get my act together very quickly.

---

## *Watch As Well As Pray*

---

You should never close both your eyes while praying; you should always keep one eye open to keep a watch for the enemy. Because he is waiting to attack when you are least expect him. Momma told us the story of when her father was in church one Sunday service and while everyone was on their knees praying, a man came in to rob the church. She said from that moment Pa John told them to "Watch As Well As Pray."

---

## *For The Old and The New*

---

There is nothing worse than being told you are going to get a whooping. But to get one for the old and the new was when you knew you were in for the long haul. And there was nothing to prepare you for the twenty-five minute whooping. It would be 3 to 6 months before I would get in trouble again. Because there was a long time between whoopings, I knew that I was going to get a killing; especially since she had allowed me to get away with things that I knew I should have already gotten a beaten for. Boy when Momma got fed up with me I was in big trouble; even Jesus could not help me no matter how much I prayed. Talking 'bout Lord let this cup pass from me; well I was having one of those moments. She would tell me, "I'm gonna beat you *for the old and the new*, borrowed and the blue. It

---

71

seemed as if I was being beaten like Jesus for hours on end, I would rather be nailed to the cross. The whooping would go something like this:

Momma: Didn't – I – tell – you – that – I – was – gonna – whoop – yo – be – hind?

Me: Yes – M'am – Momma – I – ain't – gonna – do – it – no – more!

Momma: Yes – you – are – don't – lie – to – me!

In my mind I'm telling her what she wants to hear so that she would stop. But the more I told her what she wanted to hear, she just kept on whooping me, and she didn't stop until she got tired.

## *That's Yo Lil' Red Wagon*

You had to learn to take ownership of your problems and when you would try to deny your part in the mess, Momma would tell us, *"That's yo lil' red wagon,* you mize well let the wheel keep on turning and don't stop here."

## *Laziness Hugging and Kissing You*

The nine kids my mother had all went through this, Mom would tell us to do something and she expected that we would move expeditiously. However, if we did not move when we were asked, she would yell out to us, "That ain't nothing but *laziness hugging and kissing* all over you." It never failed, especially if she had to repeat herself two or three times to get things done.

## *The Lord Will*

---

The song writer wrote "Like a ship that's tossed and driven, battered by an angry sea, the Lord will make away somehow, the Lord will make away somehow." Whenever Mom was going through something and she needed a breakthrough, she had this habit of singing while cleaning. Her singing was her way of praying and asking God to make away. Also, whenever someone was going through and one of the kids came to the house to complain about the situation, she would tell us "Keep your head up and know that *the Lord will* make away somehow." But in spite of the issues that she was having, Momma always took the time out to listen to other's problems, issues and circumstances, while she waited on God to handle hers. My mother learned this from her mother. My eldest sister Annie has a

---

letter from my grandmother telling my mom that the Lord will make a way somehow.

## *If You Don't Sit Down*

My eldest sister, Annie, told me that whenever her and my other sisters and brothers would get unruly, Momma would tell them, *"If you don't sit down*, I'm gonna beat you like Patty did the drunk." Now of course you know somebody had to ask what that meant, "I'm gonna beatcha yo ass," she said. Once that was clarified we all were quiet as mice.

## *Fair Weather Friends*

---

Momma would tell us,

> *Like the tide of the ocean coming in and going out, these are the friends that you don't need. They are only around when things are going well, but let all hell break loose and they are the first to leave. And they never offer any support and you better believe they are the first to talk about you.*

Momma simply called these folk *fair-weather friends*, not the kind to endure or last until the end.

---

## *That Black Woman*

One of God's greatest creations; there is no other like her. She's powerful and strong; most men would think God was wrong. You see she's the only one who can bear kings and queens, cook and clean, take care of the white man and have him eating out of her hand. She is that Black Woman.

## *That Black Woman*

She can take the pain whether it be through childbirth or manmade. Be it winter, spring, summer or fall, or whether it's sleet, snow, rain or sunshine, it doesn't matter she can endure them all. You see I knew a woman like this once upon a time, her name was Lois. According to II Timothy 1:5, Apostle Paul remembered the unfeigned faith of Timothy's grandmother, whose name was Lois also. I understand that Black Women are one of God's greatest creations, powerful and strong. Lois had the faith of twelve men and healing hands that were as soft as cotton, but yet had a grip that could not be forgotten.

### *That Black Woman*

Loved so great and with a heart of gold; we just never knew it ran so deeply in her soul. She was known by plenty, she touched the hearts of so many. The love that ran through her eventually took its toll on her.

### *That Black Woman*

To know her was to love her and to touch her was to feel the Holy Ghost, which was just like fire shutting up in her bones. And on that special day when she passed away, the gates of heaven opened to receive her. Oh it was a homegoing party made for one of God's Angels. There was nothing but joy, singing, shouting and dancing. I believe God took pride in his Saints that were prancing and rejoicing. There's no more tears, no more sorrow, there's no more pain there is no more tomorrow. There's nothing but love in the memory of Lois. When she jumped on that great train she didn't need a reward or recognition, only God's final admission.

## *That Black Woman*

God's Greatest Creation!

There is no other like her, she was powerful, meek, humble and strong, most men hated that God was not wrong.

# ABOUT THE AUTHOR

Lynn Brown is an inspirational writer, Ordained Minister, speaker, entrepreneur, radio announcer and President of the Broward Gospel Announcers Guild. She is a graduate of City College with a degree in Broadcast Journalism and Jacksonville Theological Seminary with a Masters degree in Christian Counseling.

Lynn realized that in the African American community and even in her own family, most children are not left an inheritance from their parents and the family ends up fighting over whatever is left. But one day Lynn realized that her mother had left her an inheritance that would last her a lifetime and it was her mother's words of wisdom.

Get this inspiring new book and identify
with *The Things Mama Used to Say*.

*Family Photo Album*

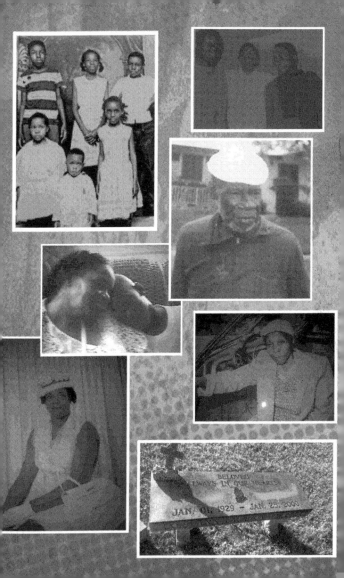

The End

Made in the USA
Columbia, SC
30 March 2021